FOR THE
VERY BUSY TECHY PASSWORD LOG

P A S S W O R D   M A N A G E R

ACTIVINOTES

Activinotes

DAILY JOURNALS, PLANNERS, NOTEBOOKS AND OTHER BLANK BOOKS

name	password update	date
website		
username		
password		
hints/notes/security question:		

name	password update	date
website		
username		
password		
hints/notes/security question:		

name	password update	date
website		
username		
password		
hints/notes/security question:		

name	password update	date
website		
username		
password		
hints/notes/security question:		

name	password update	date
website		
username		
password		
hints/notes/security question:		

name	password update	date
website		
username		
password		
hints/notes/security question:		

name	password update	date
website		
username		
password		
hints/notes/security question:		

name	password update	date
website		
username		
password		
hints/notes/security question:		

name	password update	date
website		
username		
password		
hints/notes/security question:		

name	password update	date
website		
username		
password		
hints/notes/security question:		

name	password update	date
website		
username		
password		
hints/notes/security question:		

name	password update	date
website		
username		
password		
hints/notes/security question:		

name	password update	date
website		
username		
password		
hints/notes/security question:		

name	password update	date
website		
username		
password		
hints/notes/security question:		

name	password update	date
website		
username		
password		
hints/notes/security question:		

name	password update	date
website		
username		
password		
hints/notes/security question:		

name	password update	date
website		
username		
password		
hints/notes/security question:		

name	password update	date
website		
username		
password		
hints/notes/security question:		

name	password update	date
website		
username		
password		
hints/notes/security question:		

name	password update	date
website		
username		
password		
hints/notes/security question:		

name	password update	date
website		
username		
password		
hints/notes/security question:		

name	password update	date
website		
username		
password		
hints/notes/security question:		

name	password update	date
website		
username		
password		
hints/notes/security question:		

name	password update	date
website		
username		
password		
hints/notes/security question:		

name	password update	date
website		
username		
password		
hints/notes/security question:		

name	password update	date
website		
username		
password		
hints/notes/security question:		

name	password update	date
website		
username		
password		
hints/notes/security question:		

name	password update	date
website		
username		
password		
hints/notes/security question:		

name	password update	date
website		
username		
password		
hints/notes/security question:		

name	password update	date
website		
username		
password		
hints/notes/security question:		

name	password update	date
website		
username		
password		
hints/notes/security question:		

name	password update	date
website		
username		
password		
hints/notes/security question:		

name	password update	date
website		
username		
password		
hints/notes/security question:		

name	password update	date
website		
username		
password		
hints/notes/security question:		

name	password update	date
website		
username		
password		
hints/notes/security question:		

name	password update	date
website		
username		
password		
hints/notes/security question:		

name	password update	date
website		
username		
password		
hints/notes/security question:		

name	password update	date
website		
username		
password		
hints/notes/security question:		

name	password update	date
website		
username		
password		
hints/notes/security question:		

name	password update	date
website		
username		
password		
hints/notes/security question:		

name	password update	date
website		
username		
password		
hints/notes/security question:		

name	password update	date
website		
username		
password		
hints/notes/security question:		

name	password update	date
website		
username		
password		
hints/notes/security question:		

name	password update	date
website		
username		
password		
hints/notes/security question:		

name	password update	date
website		
username		
password		
hints/notes/security question:		

name	password update	date
website		
username		
password		
hints/notes/security question:		

name	password update	date
website		
username		
password		
hints/notes/security question:		

name	password update	date
website		
username		
password		
hints/notes/security question:		

name	password update	date
website		
username		
password		
hints/notes/security question:		

name	password update	date
website		
username		
password		
hints/notes/security question:		

name	password update	date
website		
username		
password		
hints/notes/security question:		

name	password update	date
website		
username		
password		
hints/notes/security question:		

name	password update	date
website		
username		
password		
hints/notes/security question:		

name	password update	date
website		
username		
password		
hints/notes/security question:		

name	password update	date
website		
username		
password		
hints/notes/security question:		

name	password update	date
website		
username		
password		
hints/notes/security question:		

name	password update	date
website		
username		
password		
hints/notes/security question:		

name	password update	date
website		
username		
password		
hints/notes/security question:		

name	password update	date
website		
username		
password		
hints/notes/security question:		

name	password update	date
website		
username		
password		
hints/notes/security question:		

name	password update	date
website		
username		
password		
hints/notes/security question:		

name	password update	date
website		
username		
password		
hints/notes/security question:		

name	password update	date
website		
username		
password		
hints/notes/security question:		

name	password update	date
website		
username		
password		
hints/notes/security question:		

name	password update	date
website		
username		
password		
hints/notes/security question:		

name	password update	date
website		
username		
password		
hints/notes/security question:		

name	password update	date
website		
username		
password		
hints/notes/security question:		

name	password update	date
website		
username		
password		
hints/notes/security question:		

name	password update	date
website		
username		
password		
hints/notes/security question:		

name	password update	date
website		
username		
password		
hints/notes/security question:		

name	password update	date
website		
username		
password		
hints/notes/security question:		

name	password update	date
website		
username		
password		
hints/notes/security question:		

name	password update	date
website		
username		
password		
hints/notes/security question:		

name	password update	date
website		
username		
password		
hints/notes/security question:		

name	password update	date
website		
username		
password		
hints/notes/security question:		

name	password update	date
website		
username		
password		
hints/notes/security question:		

name	password update	date
website		
username		
password		
hints/notes/security question:		

name	password update	date
website		
username		
password		
hints/notes/security question:		

name	password update	date
website		
username		
password		
hints/notes/security question:		

name	password update	date
website		
username		
password		
hints/notes/security question:		

name	password update	date
website		
username		
password		
hints/notes/security question:		

name	password update	date
website		
username		
password		
hints/notes/security question:		

name	password update	date
website		
username		
password		
hints/notes/security question:		

name	password update	date
website		
username		
password		
hints/notes/security question:		

name	password update	date
website		
username		
password		
hints/notes/security question:		

name	password update	date
website		
username		
password		
hints/notes/security question:		

name	password update	date
website		
username		
password		
hints/notes/security question:		

name	password update	date
website		
username		
password		
hints/notes/security question:		

name	password update	date
website		
username		
password		
hints/notes/security question:		

name	password update	date
website		
username		
password		
hints/notes/security question:		

name	password update	date
website		
username		
password		
hints/notes/security question:		

name	password update	date
website		
username		
password		
hints/notes/security question:		

name	password update	date
website		
username		
password		
hints/notes/security question:		

name	password update	date
website		
username		
password		
hints/notes/security question:		

name	password update	date
website		
username		
password		
hints/notes/security question:		

name	password update	date
website		
username		
password		
hints/notes/security question:		

name	password update	date
website		
username		
password		
hints/notes/security question:		

name	password update	date
website		
username		
password		
hints/notes/security question:		

name	password update	date
website		
username		
password		
hints/notes/security question:		

name	password update	date
website		
username		
password		
hints/notes/security question:		

name	password update	date
website		
username		
password		
hints/notes/security question:		

name	password update	date
website		
username		
password		
hints/notes/security question:		

name	password update	date
website		
username		
password		
hints/notes/security question:		

name	password update	date
website		
username		
password		
hints/notes/security question:		

name	password update	date
website		
username		
password		
hints/notes/security question:		

name	password update	date
website		
username		
password		
hints/notes/security question:		

name	password update	date
website		
username		
password		
hints/notes/security question:		

name	password update	date
website		
username		
password		
hints/notes/security question:		

name	password update	date
website		
username		
password		
hints/notes/security question:		

name	password update	date
website		
username		
password		
hints/notes/security question:		

name	password update	date
website		
username		
password		
hints/notes/security question:		

name	password update	date
website		
username		
password		
hints/notes/security question:		

name	password update	date
website		
username		
password		
hints/notes/security question:		

name	password update	date
website		
username		
password		
hints/notes/security question:		

name	password update	date
website		
username		
password		
hints/notes/security question:		

name	password update	date
website		
username		
password		
hints/notes/security question:		

name	password update	date
website		
username		
password		
hints/notes/security question:		

name	password update	date
website		
username		
password		
hints/notes/security question:		

name	password update	date
website		
username		
password		
hints/notes/security question:		

name	password update	date
website		
username		
password		
hints/notes/security question:		

name	password update	date
website		
username		
password		
hints/notes/security question:		

name	password update	date
website		
username		
password		
hints/notes/security question:		

name	password update	date
website		
username		
password		
hints/notes/security question:		

name	password update	date
website		
username		
password		
hints/notes/security question:		

name	password update	date
website		
username		
password		
hints/notes/security question:		

name	password update	date
website		
username		
password		
hints/notes/security question:		

name	password update	date
website		
username		
password		
hints/notes/security question:		

name	password update	date
website		
username		
password		
hints/notes/security question:		

name	password update	date
website		
username		
password		
hints/notes/security question:		

name	password update	date
website		
username		
password		
hints/notes/security question:		

name	password update	date
website		
username		
password		
hints/notes/security question:		

name	password update	date
website		
username		
password		
hints/notes/security question:		

name	password update	date
website		
username		
password		
hints/notes/security question:		

name	password update	date
website		
username		
password		
hints/notes/security question:		

name	password update	date
website		
username		
password		
hints/notes/security question:		

name	password update	date
website		
username		
password		
hints/notes/security question:		

name	password update	date
website		
username		
password		
hints/notes/security question:		

name	password update	date
website		
username		
password		
hints/notes/security question:		

name	password update	date
website		
username		
password		
hints/notes/security question:		

name	password update	date
website		
username		
password		
hints/notes/security question:		

name	password update	date
website		
username		
password		
hints/notes/security question:		

name	password update	date
website		
username		
password		
hints/notes/security question:		

name	password update	date
website		
username		
password		
hints/notes/security question:		

name	password update	date
website		
username		
password		
hints/notes/security question:		

name	password update	date
website		
username		
password		
hints/notes/security question:		

name	password update	date
website		
username		
password		
hints/notes/security question:		

name	password update	date
website		
username		
password		
hints/notes/security question:		

name	password update	date
website		
username		
password		
hints/notes/security question:		

name	password update	date
website		
username		
password		
hints/notes/security question:		

name	password update	date
website		
username		
password		
hints/notes/security question:		

name	password update	date
website		
username		
password		
hints/notes/security question:		

name	password update	date
website		
username		
password		
hints/notes/security question:		

name	password update	date
website		
username		
password		
hints/notes/security question:		

name	password update	date
website		
username		
password		
hints/notes/security question:		

name	password update	date
website		
username		
password		
hints/notes/security question:		

name	password update	date
website		
username		
password		
hints/notes/security question:		

name	password update	date
website		
username		
password		
hints/notes/security question:		

name	password update	date
website		
username		
password		
hints/notes/security question:		

name	password update	date
website		
username		
password		
hints/notes/security question:		

name	password update	date
website		
username		
password		
hints/notes/security question:		

name	password update	date
website		
username		
password		
hints/notes/security question:		

name	password update	date
website		
username		
password		
hints/notes/security question:		

name	password update	date
website		
username		
password		
hints/notes/security question:		

name	password update	date
website		
username		
password		
hints/notes/security question:		

name	password update	date
website		
username		
password		
hints/notes/security question:		

name	password update	date
website		
username		
password		
hints/notes/security question:		

name	password update	date
website		
username		
password		
hints/notes/security question:		

name	password update	date
website		
username		
password		
hints/notes/security question:		

name	password update	date
website		
username		
password		
hints/notes/security question:		

name	password update	date
website		
username		
password		
hints/notes/security question:		

name	password update	date
website		
username		
password		
hints/notes/security question:		

name	password update	date
website		
username		
password		
hints/notes/security question:		

name	password update	date
website		
username		
password		
hints/notes/security question:		

name	password update	date
website		
username		
password		
hints/notes/security question:		

name	password update	date
website		
username		
password		
hints/notes/security question:		

name	password update	date
website		
username		
password		
hints/notes/security question:		

name	password update	date
website		
username		
password		
hints/notes/security question:		

name	password update	date
website		
username		
password		
hints/notes/security question:		

name	password update	date
website		
username		
password		
hints/notes/security question:		

name	password update	date
website		
username		
password		
hints/notes/security question:		

name	password update	date
website		
username		
password		
hints/notes/security question:		

name	password update	date
website		
username		
password		
hints/notes/security question:		

name	password update	date
website		
username		
password		
hints/notes/security question:		

name	password update	date
website		
username		
password		
hints/notes/security question:		

name	password update	date
website		
username		
password		
hints/notes/security question:		

name	password update	date
website		
username		
password		
hints/notes/security question:		

name	password update	date
website		
username		
password		
hints/notes/security question:		

name	password update	date
website		
username		
password		
hints/notes/security question:		

name	password update	date
website		
username		
password		
hints/notes/security question:		

name	password update	date
website		
username		
password		
hints/notes/security question:		

name	password update	date
website		
username		
password		
hints/notes/security question:		

name	password update	date
website		
username		
password		
hints/notes/security question:		

name	password update	date
website		
username		
password		
hints/notes/security question:		

name	password update	date
website		
username		
password		
hints/notes/security question:		

name	password update	date
website		
username		
password		
hints/notes/security question:		

name	password update	date
website		
username		
password		
hints/notes/security question:		

name	password update	date
website		
username		
password		
hints/notes/security question:		

name	password update	date
website		
username		
password		
hints/notes/security question:		

name	password update	date
website		
username		
password		
hints/notes/security question:		

name	password update	date
website		
username		
password		
hints/notes/security question:		

name	password update	date
website		
username		
password		
hints/notes/security question:		

name	password update	date
website		
username		
password		
hints/notes/security question:		

name	password update	date
website		
username		
password		
hints/notes/security question:		

name	password update	date
website		
username		
password		
hints/notes/security question:		

name	password update	date
website		
username		
password		
hints/notes/security question:		

name	password update	date
website		
username		
password		
hints/notes/security question:		

name	password update	date
website		
username		
password		
hints/notes/security question:		

name	password update	date
website		
username		
password		
hints/notes/security question:		

name	password update	date
website		
username		
password		
hints/notes/security question:		

name	password update	date
website		
username		
password		
hints/notes/security question:		

name	password update	date
website		
username		
password		
hints/notes/security question:		

name	password update	date
website		
username		
password		
hints/notes/security question:		

name	password update	date
website		
username		
password		
hints/notes/security question:		

name	password update	date
website		
username		
password		
hints/notes/security question:		

name	password update	date
website		
username		
password		
hints/notes/security question:		

name	password update	date
website		
username		
password		
hints/notes/security question:		

name	password update	date
website		
username		
password		
hints/notes/security question:		

name	password update	date
website		
username		
password		
hints/notes/security question:		

name	password update	date
website		
username		
password		
hints/notes/security question:		

name	password update	date
website		
username		
password		
hints/notes/security question:		

name	password update	date
website		
username		
password		
hints/notes/security question:		

name	password update	date
website		
username		
password		
hints/notes/security question:		

name	password update	date
website		
username		
password		
hints/notes/security question:		

name	password update	date
website		
username		
password		
hints/notes/security question:		

name	password update	date
website		
username		
password		
hints/notes/security question:		

name	password update	date
website		
username		
password		
hints/notes/security question:		

name	password update	date
website		
username		
password		
hints/notes/security question:		

name	password update	date
website		
username		
password		
hints/notes/security question:		

name	password update	date
website		
username		
password		
hints/notes/security question:		

name	password update	date
website		
username		
password		
hints/notes/security question:		

name	password update	date
website		
username		
password		
hints/notes/security question:		

name	password update	date
website		
username		
password		
hints/notes/security question:		

name	password update	date
website		
username		
password		
hints/notes/security question:		

name	password update	date
website		
username		
password		
hints/notes/security question:		

name	password update	date
website		
username		
password		
hints/notes/security question:		

name	password update	date
website		
username		
password		
hints/notes/security question:		

name	password update	date
website		
username		
password		
hints/notes/security question:		

name	password update	date
website		
username		
password		
hints/notes/security question:		

name	password update	date
website		
username		
password		
hints/notes/security question:		

name	password update	date
website		
username		
password		
hints/notes/security question:		

name	password update	date
website		
username		
password		
hints/notes/security question:		

name	password update	date
website		
username		
password		
hints/notes/security question:		

name	password update	date
website		
username		
password		
hints/notes/security question:		

name	password update	date
website		
username		
password		
hints/notes/security question:		

name	password update	date
website		
username		
password		
hints/notes/security question:		

name	password update	date
website		
username		
password		
hints/notes/security question:		

name	password update	date
website		
username		
password		
hints/notes/security question:		

name	password update	date
website		
username		
password		
hints/notes/security question:		

name	password update	date
website		
username		
password		
hints/notes/security question:		

name	password update	date
website		
username		
password		
hints/notes/security question:		

name	password update	date
website		
username		
password		
hints/notes/security question:		

name	password update	date
website		
username		
password		
hints/notes/security question:		

name	password update	date
website		
username		
password		
hints/notes/security question:		

name	password update	date
website		
username		
password		
hints/notes/security question:		

name	password update	date
website		
username		
password		
hints/notes/security question:		

name	password update	date
website		
username		
password		
hints/notes/security question:		

name	password update	date
website		
username		
password		
hints/notes/security question:		

name	password update	date
website		
username		
password		
hints/notes/security question:		

name	password update	date
website		
username		
password		
hints/notes/security question:		

name	password update	date
website		
username		
password		
hints/notes/security question:		

name	password update	date
website		
username		
password		
hints/notes/security question:		

name	password update	date
website		
username		
password		
hints/notes/security question:		

name	password update	date
website		
username		
password		
hints/notes/security question:		

name	password update	date
website		
username		
password		
hints/notes/security question:		

name	password update	date
website		
username		
password		
hints/notes/security question:		

name	password update	date
website		
username		
password		
hints/notes/security question:		

name	password update	date
website		
username		
password		
hints/notes/security question:		

name	password update	date
website		
username		
password		
hints/notes/security question:		

name	password update	date
website		
username		
password		
hints/notes/security question:		

name	password update	date
website		
username		
password		
hints/notes/security question:		

name	password update	date
website		
username		
password		
hints/notes/security question:		

name	password update	date
website		
username		
password		
hints/notes/security question:		

name	password update	date
website		
username		
password		
hints/notes/security question:		

name	password update	date
website		
username		
password		
hints/notes/security question:		

name	password update	date
website		
username		
password		
hints/notes/security question:		

name	password update	date
website		
username		
password		
hints/notes/security question:		

name	password update	date
website		
username		
password		
hints/notes/security question:		

name	password update	date
website		
username		
password		
hints/notes/security question:		

name	password update	date
website		
username		
password		
hints/notes/security question:		

name	password update	date
website		
username		
password		
hints/notes/security question:		

name	password update	date
website		
username		
password		
hints/notes/security question:		

name	password update	date
website		
username		
password		
hints/notes/security question:		

name	password update	date
website		
username		
password		
hints/notes/security question:		

name	password update	date
website		
username		
password		
hints/notes/security question:		

name	password update	date
website		
username		
password		
hints/notes/security question:		

name	password update	date
website		
username		
password		
hints/notes/security question:		

name	password update	date
website		
username		
password		
hints/notes/security question:		

name	password update	date
website		
username		
password		
hints/notes/security question:		

name	password update	date
website		
username		
password		
hints/notes/security question:		

name	password update	date
website		
username		
password		
hints/notes/security question:		

name	password update	date
website		
username		
password		
hints/notes/security question:		

name	password update	date
website		
username		
password		
hints/notes/security question:		

name	password update	date
website		
username		
password		
hints/notes/security question:		

name	password update	date
website		
username		
password		
hints/notes/security question:		

name	password update	date
website		
username		
password		
hints/notes/security question:		

name	password update	date
website		
username		
password		
hints/notes/security question:		

name	password update	date
website		
username		
password		
hints/notes/security question:		

name	password update	date
website		
username		
password		
hints/notes/security question:		

name	password update	date
website		
username		
password		
hints/notes/security question:		

name	password update	date
website		
username		
password		
hints/notes/security question:		

name	password update	date
website		
username		
password		
hints/notes/security question:		

name	password update	date
website		
username		
password		
hints/notes/security question:		

name	password update	date
website		
username		
password		
hints/notes/security question:		

name	password update	date
website		
username		
password		
hints/notes/security question:		

name	password update	date
website		
username		
password		
hints/notes/security question:		

name	password update	date
website		
username		
password		
hints/notes/security question:		

name	password update	date
website		
username		
password		
hints/notes/security question:		

name	password update	date
website		
username		
password		
hints/notes/security question:		

name	password update	date
website		
username		
password		
hints/notes/security question:		

name	password update	date
website		
username		
password		
hints/notes/security question:		

name	password update	date
website		
username		
password		
hints/notes/security question:		

name	password update	date
website		
username		
password		
hints/notes/security question:		

name	password update	date
website		
username		
password		
hints/notes/security question:		

name	password update	date
website		
username		
password		
hints/notes/security question:		

name	password update	date
website		
username		
password		
hints/notes/security question:		

name	password update	date
website		
username		
password		
hints/notes/security question:		

name	password update	date
website		
username		
password		
hints/notes/security question:		

name	password update	date
website		
username		
password		
hints/notes/security question:		

name	password update	date
website		
username		
password		
hints/notes/security question:		

name	password update	date
website		
username		
password		
hints/notes/security question:		

name	password update	date
website		
username		
password		
hints/notes/security question:		

name	password update	date
website		
username		
password		
hints/notes/security question:		

name	password update	date
website		
username		
password		
hints/notes/security question:		

name	password update	date
website		
username		
password		
hints/notes/security question:		

name	password update	date
website		
username		
password		
hints/notes/security question:		

name	password update	date
website		
username		
password		
hints/notes/security question:		

name	password update	date
website		
username		
password		
hints/notes/security question:		

name	password update	date
website		
username		
password		
hints/notes/security question:		

name	password update	date
website		
username		
password		
hints/notes/security question:		

name	password update	date
website		
username		
password		
hints/notes/security question:		

name	password update	date
website		
username		
password		
hints/notes/security question:		

name	password update	date
website		
username		
password		
hints/notes/security question:		

name	password update	date
website		
username		
password		
hints/notes/security question:		

name	password update	date
website		
username		
password		
hints/notes/security question:		

name	password update	date
website		
username		
password		
hints/notes/security question:		

name	password update	date
website		
username		
password		
hints/notes/security question:		

name	password update	date
website		
username		
password		
hints/notes/security question:		

name	password update	date
website		
username		
password		
hints/notes/security question:		

name	password update	date
website		
username		
password		
hints/notes/security question:		

name	password update	date
website		
username		
password		
hints/notes/security question:		

name	password update	date
website		
username		
password		
hints/notes/security question:		

name	password update	date
website		
username		
password		
hints/notes/security question:		

name	password update	date
website		
username		
password		
hints/notes/security question:		

name	password update	date
website		
username		
password		
hints/notes/security question:		

name	password update	date
website		
username		
password		
hints/notes/security question:		

name	password update	date
website		
username		
password		
hints/notes/security question:		

name	password update	date
website		
username		
password		
hints/notes/security question:		

name	password update	date
website		
username		
password		
hints/notes/security question:		

name	password update	date
website		
username		
password		
hints/notes/security question:		

name	password update	date
website		
username		
password		
hints/notes/security question:		

name	password update	date
website		
username		
password		
hints/notes/security question:		

name	password update	date
website		
username		
password		
hints/notes/security question:		

name	password update	date
website		
username		
password		
hints/notes/security question:		

name	password update	date
website		
username		
password		
hints/notes/security question:		

name	password update	date
website		
username		
password		
hints/notes/security question:		

name	password update	date
website		
username		
password		
hints/notes/security question:		

name	password update	date
website		
username		
password		
hints/notes/security question:		

name	password update	date
website		
username		
password		
hints/notes/security question:		

name	password update	date
website		
username		
password		
hints/notes/security question:		

name	password update	date
website		
username		
password		
hints/notes/security question:		

name	password update	date
website		
username		
password		
hints/notes/security question:		

name	password update	date
website		
username		
password		
hints/notes/security question:		

name	password update	date
website		
username		
password		
hints/notes/security question:		

name	password update	date
website		
username		
password		
hints/notes/security question:		

name	password update	date
website		
username		
password		
hints/notes/security question:		

name	password update	date
website		
username		
password		
hints/notes/security question:		

name	password update	date
website		
username		
password		
hints/notes/security question:		

name	password update	date
website		
username		
password		
hints/notes/security question:		

name	password update	date
website		
username		
password		
hints/notes/security question:		

name	password update	date
website		
username		
password		
hints/notes/security question:		

name	password update	date
website		
username		
password		
hints/notes/security question:		

name	password update	date
website		
username		
password		
hints/notes/security question:		

name	password update	date
website		
username		
password		
hints/notes/security question:		

name	password update	date
website		
username		
password		
hints/notes/security question:		

name	password update	date
website		
username		
password		
hints/notes/security question:		

name	password update	date
website		
username		
password		
hints/notes/security question:		

name	password update	date
website		
username		
password		
hints/notes/security question:		

name	password update	date
website		
username		
password		
hints/notes/security question:		

name	password update	date
website		
username		
password		
hints/notes/security question:		

name	password update	date
website		
username		
password		
hints/notes/security question:		

name	password update	date
website		
username		
password		
hints/notes/security question:		

name	password update	date
website		
username		
password		
hints/notes/security question:		

name	password update	date
website		
username		
password		
hints/notes/security question:		

name	password update	date
website		
username		
password		
hints/notes/security question:		

name	password update	date
website		
username		
password		
hints/notes/security question:		

name	password update	date
website		
username		
password		
hints/notes/security question:		

name	password update	date
website		
username		
password		
hints/notes/security question:		

name	password update	date
website		
username		
password		
hints/notes/security question:		

name	password update	date
website		
username		
password		
hints/notes/security question:		

name	password update	date
website		
username		
password		
hints/notes/security question:		

name	password update	date
website		
username		
password		
hints/notes/security question:		

name	password update	date
website		
username		
password		
hints/notes/security question:		

name	password update	date
website		
username		
password		
hints/notes/security question:		

name	password update	date
website		
username		
password		
hints/notes/security question:		

name	password update	date
website		
username		
password		
hints/notes/security question:		

name	password update	date
website		
username		
password		
hints/notes/security question:		

name	password update	date
website		
username		
password		
hints/notes/security question:		

name	password update	date
website		
username		
password		
hints/notes/security question:		

name	password update	date
website		
username		
password		
hints/notes/security question:		

name	password update	date
website		
username		
password		
hints/notes/security question:		

name	password update	date
website		
username		
password		
hints/notes/security question:		

name	password update	date
website		
username		
password		
hints/notes/security question:		

name	password update	date
website		
username		
password		
hints/notes/security question:		

name	password update	date
website		
username		
password		
hints/notes/security question:		

name	password update	date
website		
username		
password		
hints/notes/security question:		

name	password update	date
website		
username		
password		
hints/notes/security question:		

name	password update	date
website		
username		
password		
hints/notes/security question:		

name	password update	date
website		
username		
password		
hints/notes/security question:		

name	password update	date
website		
username		
password		
hints/notes/security question:		

name	password update	date
website		
username		
password		
hints/notes/security question:		

name	password update	date
website		
username		
password		
hints/notes/security question:		

name	password update	date
website		
username		
password		
hints/notes/security question:		

name	password update	date
website		
username		
password		
hints/notes/security question:		

name	password update	date
website		
username		
password		
hints/notes/security question:		

name	password update	date
website		
username		
password		
hints/notes/security question:		

name	password update	date
website		
username		
password		
hints/notes/security question:		

www.ingramcontent.com/pod-product-compliance
Lightning Source LLC
Chambersburg PA
CBHW081334090426
42737CB00017B/3136